HOW TO GET A JOB IN 90 DAYS

7 STEPS TO BECOMING A JOB MAGNET

PENDIUM
PUBLISHING HOUSE
514-201 DANIELS STREET
RALEIGH, NC 27605

For information, please visit our Web site at
www.pendiumpublishing.com

PENDIUM Publishing and its logo
are registered trademarks.

How to Get a Job in 90 Days
7 Steps to Becoming a Job Magnet
by CJ Gross

Copyright © CJ Gross, 2014
All Rights Reserved.

ISBN: 978-1-936513-95-6

PUBLISHER'S NOTE

Without limiting the rights under the copyright reserved above, no part of this publication may be reproduced, stored in or introduced into a retrieval system, or transmitted, in any form, or by any means (electronic, mechanical, photocopying, recording, or otherwise), without the prior written permission of both the copyright owner and the above publisher of this book.

If you purchased this book without a cover you should be aware that the book is stolen property. It was reported as "unsold and destroyed" to the publisher and neither the author nor the publisher has received any payment for this "stripped book."

This book is printed on acid-free paper.

HOW TO GET A JOB IN 90 DAYS

7 STEPS TO BECOMING A JOB MAGNET

CJ GROSS
THE RELATIONSHIP ENGINEER

ACKNOWLEDGMENTS

I want to acknowledge and thank my parents, Ella J. Gross and John Gross, who taught me the importance of working hard, persevering, and believing in myself. To my daughters, Phallen Cummings, and Christen and Lauren Gross, thank you for supporting my business and being my motivation for success.

Thank you to all of my former employers and managers for allowing me to gain valuable knowledge to help me in my career.

Thank you to Lori Gross and Nikki Harley for helping me stay focused on this book and its completion.

Thank you to my editorial team, Kay Shopskire, Teresa Hamilton, Doc Wilson, Angela Garett and Janice Cummings.

Thank you to Mark Victor Hansen and Robert G. Allen, the authors of *"The One Minute Millionaire: The Enlightened Way to Wealth,"* which was the inspiration for the conception and development of this book.

Thank you to everyone who has supported me through purchasing this book, or hiring me as a speaker.

CONTENTS

Acknowledgments v

Chapter 1: Introduction 1
Chapter 2: The Job Magnet Philosophy 3
Chapter 3: Step #1: Know Thyself 5
Chapter 4: Step #2: Target the Right Job 14
Chapter 5: Step #3: Discover Your Unique
 Selling Advantage 19
Chapter 6: Step #4: Develop a Resume That
 Tells a Great Story About You 29
Chapter 7: Step #5: Develop Your Network 42
Chapter 8: Step #6: Dress for the Response! 49
Chapter 9: Step #7: Ace That Interview 56
Chapter 10: The 90-Day Game Plan 75
Chapter 11: So You Want to be a Job Magnet? 80

About the Author 83

A PERSPECTIVE

Always define WHAT you want to do with your life, and WHAT you have to offer to the world, in terms of your favorite talents, gifts, and skills - not in terms of a job title.
— Richard Nelson Bolles, What Color Is Your Parachute? 2007: A Practical Manual for Job-Hunters and Career-Changers

CHAPTER 1

Introduction

Hello Future Job Magnets!

For many years, I have conducted workshops and provided coaching on the topic of "How to get a job in 90 days, and how to become a job magnet." You're probably thinking "What makes him think he can teach me," or "What makes HIM an expert on this?" Well, the answer is clear, and, I might add, very simple. I can make these statements because of my extensive experience, from which I developed confidence, assurance, validation, and expertise. Do you think it's too simplistic? I believe that you would fully understand if you knew how I started as a timid fellow, and then developed into an individual who knew that I finally had the power to pursue my professional interests – knowing all along that I absolutely would attain my goal! No question whatsoever!

Several years ago, over the course of a week, five different companies each offered me a job. When one of my friends asked me how did I get so many job offers, I replied "I got them because I am a Job Magnet!" After we had several in-depth, long discussions, and he had studied and observed my approach to getting hired, he encouraged me to share my techniques and abilities with others. He suggested that I conduct a workshop on the topic to help others who were struggling with the interview process and unable to land a job.

Now, possessing confidence in your own abilities is one thing, but feeling that you can instill a similar response in another human being is a different matter! But self-assurance won out, and I did a workshop at a local library. It was a huge hit! Imagine my surprise at the large number of people who showed up – hoping that they, too, could learn the secrets of becoming Job Magnets!

Since then, I have been helping virtually everyone who is open to receiving my message. I have succeeded not only in helping those who lacked skills, education, training, and motivation, but also those who had high levels of education, experience, motivation, and training. I helped numerous individuals develop confidence and land good jobs. After conducting hundreds of workshops, and providing many hours of both group and one-on-one coaching, I decided to write this book in order to reach the widest audience possible, and thus to have a greater impact in preparing people to land great jobs. Finally, it is abundantly clear that local economies, as well as the national economy, would benefit greatly from having better matching between job skill requirements and the skills of those applying for those jobs.

Before you can fully comprehend the concepts, the steps, the required actions, and the truisms of this book, you must first realize that diligently applying all of these elements cannot – in and of themselves – make you into a Job Magnet. First, you must study, understand, and embrace the components of The Job Magnet Philosophy, which provides the foundation upon which a true Job Magnet is built. Continue to Chapter 2 for this part of the program!

CHAPTER 2

The Job Magnet Philosophy

Generally, to understand The Job Magnet Philosophy, you need to comprehend and fully embrace the truism that you – and you alone – control your future and your destiny. This critical concept is all-encompassing, and stresses the importance of gaining self-knowledge, and devoting the required time and attention for study and immersion training, as well as developing a single-minded dedication to excellence and achievement.

The following is a list of **The 10 Beliefs and Competencies** that must become your mantra as you begin the process of transforming yourself into a Job Magnet:

- Companies are looking for me, not just someone like me – but actually <u>ME</u>!
- I have a unique selling advantage that others do not possess, and I know exactly what it is.
- I fully deserve the job I want.
- I am willing to work incredibly hard to get the job I want.
- I am willing to talk to as many people as are necessary to get the job I want.
- I am willing to take extra classes and training to get the job I want.

- I am will dedicate time, energy, money, and focus to learn more about my desired industry.
- I am willing to become an expert in the industry in which I want to work.
- I am willing to do all of the activities in this book to get the job I want.
- I am great, and I hold the keys to my destiny.

Before you finish reading this book, you would benefit strongly from taking time to memorize and understand The Job Magnet Philosophy above. Read and repeat the philosophy several times until it becomes a part of your thought processes and your belief about finding a job.

Whatever the mind can conceive and believe, it can achieve. - Napoleon Hill, author of *Think and Grow Rich*

CHAPTER 3

Step #1: Know Thyself

One of the most important things you need to know about the job magnet process is in-depth information about the product you are going to market: **YOU!!!** You need to know your talents, your skills, and your innate abilities. When you are a job magnet, you will know better who you are, what you do well, the areas you need to improve upon, and what you want out of your work experience.

When recruiters and hiring managers are looking to hire, they are looking for someone who has a sense of purpose for their life's work, and who knows how that purpose can fit into their particular company. In order to properly sell you and your skills to a company, you must know YOU!

Knowing yourself requires the ability and desire to understand yourself on many levels, or at least as many levels as you can handle for the time being. Also, you must be curious about yourself, and be willing to learn to see yourself through the eyes of others. In addition, you must be willing to peel back your insulating layers of security so that you can get to your true north – which is the direction you want to move toward in your life and in your career. To be truthful, this can be a painful process, but it is a process that has to be done.

So, let's get started with the trait that can make or break

– and overshadow – all of your successes relative to your other traits.

Temperament

Understanding your temperament is the first step to address on your journey to better understanding yourself. Your temperament is an innate psychological trait - a predisposition with which you were born. It is a part of the fabric of your physical, mental, and spiritual matrix. Recognizing and understanding the specific attributes of your temperament will allow you to better utilize your temperament not only to land certain jobs, but also to become super successful in those jobs. This will give you a decisive advantage over others such that you will be much more likely to make it to the top of the pile of job seekers for most jobs.

How do you figure out temperament and all of its relevant traits? Getting a handle on your temperament is relatively easy because you can gage your temperament with the help of a tested and proven scientific tool specifically designed for this purpose. For this purpose, I highly recommend the Keirsey Temperament Sorter®-II (KTS®-II) test.

[**NOTE:** The Keirsey Temperament Sorter®-II (KTS®-II) test is one of the most widely used personality assessment instruments in the world. It uses a powerful seventy-question questionnaire to help individuals discover their personality type. The KTS-II is based on the **Keirsey Temperament Theory™,** which has been published in the 2 best-selling books, *"Please Understand Me,"* and *"Please Understand Me II,"* by David West Keirsey, PhD. The KTS-II links human behavioral patterns to four temperaments and sixteen character types. Dr. Keirsey was an American psychologist, a professor emeritus at California

State University, Fullerton, and the author of several books. He specialized in family and partnership counseling, and the coaching of children and adults. You can study and take the Keirsey Temperament assessment at www.keirsey.com.]

Character

It is also important to understand character. The components of character include integrity, trust, honesty, loyalty, resilience, respect, responsibility, and self-confidence. Also, in character you sometimes can find greater or lesser amounts of the negative traits of hopelessness, selfishness, dishonesty, and envy. You can learn and unlearn character. You may learn components of character through various life situations and through both consistent and inconsistent relationships. Since character can be learned and unlearned, clearly you can choose the traits you desire, and throw away the traits that are displeasing to your friends, family, and coworkers, or that are holding you back from becoming the person that you want to be. In addition, you can develop your character by reading personal development books and biographies of great leaders, and by becoming involved in leadership programs that require you to associate with mentors that have a good moral compass.

> *"It is your character, and your character alone, that will make your life happy or unhappy. That is all that really passes for destiny. And you choose it. No one else can give it to you or deny it to you. No rival can steal it from you. And no friend can give it to you. Others can encourage you to make the right choices or discourage you. But you choose."* – John McCain, US Senator.

Character is what a man is in the dark. – Dwight L. Moody, preacher, evangelist, and publisher,

The best index to a person's character is how he treats people who can't do him any good, and how he treats people who can't fight back. – Abigail Van Buren, columnist for "Dear Abby."

Personality

Your personality reflects how your temperament and character are expressed around others. Your personality allows you to negotiate with both your temperament and your character to fit into or meet the expectation of the social environment to which we desire acceptance. Personality is the culmination of different psychological components of a person and to some degree represents how we see ourselves. Your personality can show in how you present yourself. For instance, the type of clothes you wear, your hairstyle, and the type of jewelry you wear, all reflect your personality.

> *"Personality is what judges a person and makes him. It is beauty that captures your attention, personality that captures your heart. Personality has the capability to break all barriers and emerge as the shining star; it comes out of the physical flaws and the actions and shines as a crowning glory. Personality is unique to every person. Even if you try to imitate, your personality will make you different from others. Paul Harris once said, 'Personality has the power to uplift, power to depress, power to curse and the power to bless. In order to develop your personality, you have*

> *to develop traits that will be unique to you and give a name and fame. It is like the fragrance of a flower. The fragrance of a flower is unique to the flower; likewise, personality identifies you. So, improve on the traits that define you and enhance your personality."*
>
> -Author unknown

Your personality can determine whether you get a job, your character can determine whether you keep the job, and your temperament can determine whether you are going to be great at the job.

How We See the World

Most people view the world from the perspectives of their temperament and their character. It is very natural to look at situations from the perspective of your experiences and values (which have contributed to your character) and your innate temperament. But you must ask yourself ***"how do I use my temperament to connect with others?"*** *You* must know and accept your temperament in order to better understand how it affects the way you view certain situations and actions of others. Once you are familiar with your own temperament, and understand the temperament of others at a good level, you can better solve relationship and business challenges.

So, what are the benefits of understanding temperament? When you understand temperament, you have increased knowledge of self, more effective communication skills, increased self-confidence, higher productivity, and the ability to achieve faster success.

Let me use a personal example here. At one point in my life, I had to have a talk with myself. "Why am I working as a mechanical designer in the engineering field? This is not me!" I felt very out of place and unfulfilled. However, I realized that, subconsciously, I was seeking something to give my life a sense of meaning and purpose. To that end, a few days later I found an audio program in the library entitled *"You Can Do Anything You Want if You Just Know What it Is"* by Barbara Smith. After answering the questions on the audio program, I realized that I was good at working with people. In addition to answering the questions on the audio program, I took several personality tests, one of which was the Keirsey Temperament Sorter – mentioned above.

The results of the temperament assessment amazed me, to say the least. It was like the assessment captured the very thoughts running through my mind – including my perceptions on business, work, and personal matters. It was so accurate that I found it scary. After compiling the information from various assessment tests and from some coaching, I decided to transform my life to fit my temperament and personality type. I researched jobs that I could apply for with my limited experience, but that also utilized my newfound knowledge of purpose and my ability to work well with people.

Then, I did two main things to help me develop and showcase my skills of working with people. First, I started a mentoring program at the engineering firm I was currently employed with. Second, in my spare time, I started a mentoring program in my community. This allowed me to showcase my talents, and also give back to the community that had helped support me. I created a picture book that highlighted the activities of the mentoring program, and also added both mentoring programs to my resume under work experience. I then submitted my resume for jobs with several entities, and was hired at a juvenile facility in Maryland, where I taught drafting and business skills. In addition, I added life skills because that area was a critical part of my new transformation. It was a lot of work, it took a lot of time, and it demanded a lot of perseverance from me; however, in the end, it afforded some great rewards. You see, on top of getting a job that allowed me to work directly with others, I also received a $10,000 pay increase! This one job propelled me in my new career direction of helping people, and also provided a platform for launching my coaching and training business – fulfilling a mission that I conduct to this day.

Homework Activity: Personal Inventory

Lists can be great tools to have at your fingertips. You know – the "To-Do List," the "Grocery List," the "Bucket List," etc. Not only do they remind you of things you need to do and help keep you on track, but they also provide structure to your busy, ever-changing life. They can be simple, brief, and even written on the back of a chewing gum wrapper or on the palm of your hand! They are useful, and you can save them for the purpose of comparing and looking at trends – over time – such as, how thoroughly you completed them, and other revealing analyses.

Let's do an activity. Create a list of things that you believe you are skilled in, and that you believe people or companies would pay you to do, such as typing, speaking, repairing computers, teaching, sewing, editing, coaching, and so forth (your **"My Skills List"**). Then create a second list of things that you like to do, but things for which you lack the skills or training necessary to be proficient (your **"My Likes List"**). Next, create a third list of abilities that you believe you were born with (your **My Talents List"**). Highlight or circle the skills and talents that you are drawn to, and the ones you have noticed others in the workplace are drawn to. [**NOTE:** A **skill** is something that you are proficient in, and a **talent** is something that you are naturally gifted in.] These 3 lists are important because they help you understand what areas will more easily make you a Job Magnet, and what areas you need to develop a higher proficiency level to make you an even better one.

Finally, ask your friends and co-workers to create a list of things that they believe you are skilled in, and that they believe people or companies would pay you to do (your **"Friends' Skills List"**). Again, highlight or circle the skills and talents that you are drawn to, and the ones you have noticed in others in the workplace. Then compare and combine your **Friends' Skills List** with the 3 lists you created above, and just highlight skills and talents that surface on more than one list (your **"Combined List"**). Then use your **Combined List** as a guide to help you determine the right career field for you. Also, take as many Skills Assessments and Personal Inventories as you can find on the Internet, and consult career counseling and career coaching books and Internet sources. Compiling and comparing such data will help you fine tune your **Combined List** so that you will be better able to see the strong and clear direction in which you *really* want your professional career to go.

Next Step. What education, training, and other experiences have you had that will help you become a job magnet? Create a list of your degrees and certifications, workshops/seminars you've attended, e-courses you've taken, and even books you've read (your **"Education List"**). This list will help you see the "collective training" you have experienced, and possibly what skills you may need to hone to look more enticing as a Job Magnet.

Next Step. Create a list of areas in which you, and/or others, believe you are an expert or even a genius (your **"Expert List"**). This will also be called **your unique selling advantage**.

Collectively, the above lists that you have created will help you to move forward with authority and confidence as you develop your resume, partake in networking, and – most of all – become a Job Magnet.

Final Step. Create a list of the things you absolutely hate to do (your **"Hate To Do List"**). This list can come from your past or present work experiences or from other aspects of your life until now. This list will help you steer clear of jobs that require you to perform too many tasks that will make you miserable, and possibly result in your company being unimpressed with your work performance. In addition, this information will help you to develop better self-awareness, and help you to more quickly become a Job Magnet.

Remember, **your unique selling advantage** allows you to gain leverage both in the job market and in the interview. Knowing your unique selling advantage, and how to articulate it, are also critical for your success in your job hunt, as well as in your development as you become a Job Magnet.

CHAPTER 4

Step #2: Target the Right Job

It is critical for you to target the right job because it will help ensure that you are barking up the right tree, and moving strategically in the right career and job direction. It would make no sense for you to apply for jobs that you don't really want, or jobs that don't really want you. Finding the right job is similar to dating in that both parties must be interested.

To become the most effective, powerful Job Magnet, you must identify available jobs that are congruent with your skill sets and, most importantly, your temperament. Such job positions are called **Congruent Positions** when they are in line with both your temperament and your skill set. It is extremely important that you look for jobs that are as congruent as possible. These are the jobs that you will find the easiest to land, and the jobs in which you will be the most effective and the happiest.

You also want to identify companies that support the kind of work environment that meets your psycho/social needs. These companies are called **Congruent Companies.** For example, these companies might have great benefits, in-house gyms, daycare, etc., or they may allow their employees to work from home or have flexible hours. Your **Congruent Company** might also have travel opportunities, educational reimbursement, or a stellar reputation for strong upward mobility opportunities. In your opinion, whatever qualities make a company a great place to work - including highly valuing the skills and talents of each of its employees – makes it a **Congruent Company.** In addition, **Congruent Companies** are looking to hire people **just like you** – that is, people with **your skill sets** and **your personality and temperament!** In short, **these Companies want you!!!**

Finding the Right Job So That You Are Not the Wrong Employee

According to *"The American Time Use Survey,"* conducted by the United States Bureau of Labor in 2012, Americans between the ages of 25 and 54 spent more time working than any other activity. If you are going to spend most of your life working, then shouldn't you spend most of that time working in a job that is perfect for you!? There is nothing worse than the right employee in the wrong job! Let me repeat that:

> *"There is nothing worse than the right employee in the wrong job!"*

Let me explain. The "right" employee looks right, and has the right experience and education; but what makes him the wrong employee is his/her intent – most often, money and status. Don't waste your time focusing on finding jobs that simply will earn you more money – for such jobs usually will carry the extreme risk of bringing you boat loads of misery and unhappiness.

In his ground breaking book *"Flow,"* Mihaly Csikszentmihali, a Hungarian Psychology professor, revealed that those who worked in jobs that fit their personality and skill set, and that challenged their abilities and supported some of their core values, were far happier than those who worked primarily for money. Although working for bigger money is a necessity for many people – and possibly including you, you should always strive to align yourself with a job that fits your personality and skill set, challenges your abilities, and supports some, if not all, of your core values.

In 1943, Abraham Maslow, an American Psychologist, published a paper entitled *"A Theory of Human Motivation,"* in which he presented his theory that people cannot truly grow and develop until they get their basic needs met. He theorized that, only once a person's basic needs were met, could they develop into their higher, creative self. It is evident that sometimes you might have to make sacrifices to pay your various bills; however, generally speaking, you should always be moving toward the right job so that you don't run the risk of becoming complacent, disgruntled or trapped in a job or career that is not right for you. In other words, if you take a job solely to meet your basic needs for an extended period of time – without considering your personality, your skill set, and your core values – you most likely are working for the wrong employer, and will not be happy in the long run.

A Perspective on Money

Money is nothing more than value represented as numbers dyed on cotton and linen fibers. Its owner uses it to trade for something else that he/she believes a worthwhile exchange. The more value you bring to the workplace, the more money you will make in any career field. Since money aligns with the value its owner decides, you don't have to look for it; rather, money will find you if you bring value to the marketplace. The best way to bring value to the market place is to only accept the right job; this way, you will find both the money you seek AND happiness!

Let me use another personal example here. When I used my experience in both the engineering and the social services fields as a basis for applying for a hybrid job, I was able to land a job with the Washington, D.C., Department of Parks and Recreation. This position allowed me to use my general people skills (including my diplomatic skills) in an urban environment in which I engaged and made presentations to, political leaders in the community. This position provided the great platform from which, ultimately, I was transformed into a Job Magnet. I became a much sought-after leader in my community, and my services were engaged by multiple organizations. If I had not found such a "right" position, I would not have excelled to the magnificent extent that I did! This job gave me the freedom to express myself, and brought me much needed success – primarily from me exploring myself in newfound ways that produced a deeper understanding of myself. In addition, this job helped me develop some of my God-given talents that I had not recognized before!

> Do not hire a man who does your work for money, but him who does it for love of it.
> - Henry David Thoreau, American author, poet, and philosopher.

Homework Activity: Research

Your mini research project is to use the Internet to identify a dozen or more companies with which you are congruent. You can start by selecting one of the many available search engines (Google, Yahoo!, etc.). Type in such words as "best place to work," and then add your state, your city, and even your particular industry. Then, conduct a more in-depth examination of 3 or 4 of the companies that are at the top of the resulting list. Be sure to check each company's available jobs. Another research direction might include asking a few employees of those companies how they like their company.

Yet another approach would be to attend industry seminars, conferences, and association meetings. At such events, you would make it your prime purpose to meet people who work for companies that are congruent to you. These networking opportunities often will reveal unique information about those companies, including hiring opportunities that may not yet have been advertised, or that will become available in the future. Just think: You might even get a job interview (and maybe even the job!) before the company advertises the job!!!

Also, be certain to check as many of the job search engines as you can, such as Indeed, Beyond, The Leader, Snagajob, Jobs.com, Monster, Link Up, and USA Jobs for companies that are looking for people with your skill set. In addition, constantly and consistently ask every person you meet where they work and if they like their job (if they work for a company that is congruent to you).

I guarantee that this activity will help you identify the best job opportunities to give you the greatest probability of finding the meaningful and fulfilling employment that you seek!

CHAPTER 5

Step #3: Discover Your Unique Selling Advantage

If you have ever been in a good sales training course, you may have heard the term "Unique Selling Advantage." A Unique Selling Advantage is a particular advantage a product has over other similar products. For example, if there are five million widgets on the market, what makes this widget unique compared to the other five million widgets (minus one!)? What does it do that the others don't? How will this knowledge benefit me? These are the types of questions you will have to answer if you want to become a Job Magnet. Basically, what makes you unique and what sets you apart from the rest? It almost gives you superhero status. All superheroes have a specific power that separates them from other superheroes, and that helps them defeat the villains. Without this super power, they would be regular people with no power. No one would ever read about them because they would not be perceived as unique or outstanding, and perhaps not even interesting. Your Unique Selling Advantage is why recruiters and hiring managers would read your resume; they would find you interesting and want to know more about you and your story. They would want your "superpowers" in their company, and hiring managers want you in their department and on their team. And there'd be a good chance that they would be willing to pay top dollar for you!

People who have a Unique Selling Advantage are natural Job Magnets because they attract employers. Job Magnets do not have to look for jobs; on the contrary, jobs look for them! Your Unique Selling Advantage separates you from the masses, and distinguishes you from someone who just meets the minimum requirements.

Your Unique Selling Advantage will include several things, and is comprised of your innate talent, your skill set, your temperament, your personality, your knowledge of your chosen field, and – most importantly – your ability to articulate your philosophy in written and verbal communication.

Your Innate Talent

Let's talk about your innate talent. Your innate talent is your ability to do something naturally without being taught, without formal training, and, many times, without previous experience. This is what some people call a gift from God. Knowing your gift can be extremely helpful in your job search. Knowing your gift can also help you choose what type of schooling and training you need, and what career path will be best suited for you. For example, if your innate talent is math, then you might choose to go to school in any of a variety of areas, such as engineering, teaching, finance, or business. On the other hand, if your innate talent is working with people, you might choose to go to school for counseling, job training, or social work. Or, if your innate talent is working with your hands, then you might want to consider going to school for automotive repair or carpentry. Innate talents are endless.

If you choose not to go to school, then you might want to consider finding an apprenticeship program or a mentor who would help develop your talents into a marketable skill. An apprenticeship program is great because it allows you to earn while you learn. You can make money while you are learning how to sharpen your skills. Apprenticeships may also prepare you for exams, certifications, and licenses. A mentor can also assist you in developing yourself, avoiding career pitfalls, and learning other nuances that would help you grow tremendously in your chosen career path.

Your Skill Set

Your skill set is the things that you can do well, or things in which you are proficient. If you can put together a spreadsheet or a PowerPoint presentation, and teach others to do the same, then you are skilled and proficient in PowerPoint presentations. Typically, your skills are developed over time by making mistakes, and then learning (or otherwise figuring out) how to move past those mistakes to gain competency. When you are skilled at something – whether or not you like doing it, you can offer it as one of your Unique Selling Advantages.

Your Temperament

Your temperament is comprised of specific inherent attributes that are as natural as breathing. Your in-depth knowledge of them will help you better understand the power of your Unique Selling Advantage. You can read more about temperaments and take the Keirsey Temperament Assessment questionnaire at www.keirsey.com.

Your Personality

Your personality is the combination of your temperament and your character. Some companies look for certain personality types for certain jobs – especially when the jobs require working with people. On the other hand, working alone requires yet another type of personality. Either way, when you understand your personality type, you will better understand the power of your Unique Selling Advantage, and how to harness that power. You will be able to find a number of personality assessment tests from an on-line search. I recommend that you take as many of these tests as you can, and study and contrast your results.

Your Knowledge of Your Chosen Career Field

Knowledge of your chosen career field is extremely important for enhancing and enriching your Unique Selling Advantage. Knowledge of your chosen career field is different from your work experiences. Your work experience is what jobs you have done in your career, and your career field knowledge is what you have learned in your career field while working in those jobs. You could have had many great jobs, yet not have gained an appreciable amount of knowledge about your industry. Consider all you know about your chosen career field and industry as *knowledge equity* – which you can cash out during an interview, or, with luck, at the time of salary negotiations!

Your Ability to Articulate Your Philosophy in Written and Verbal Communications

Every Job Magnet has their unique philosophy about their career field. Your philosophy is comprised of your understanding of:

- your chosen career field and industry,
- the industry's best practices,
- the nuances that makes a person successful in your chosen career field and industry,
- the philosophy of successful people in your field,
- your individual guiding principles, and,
- most importantly, your unique perceptions as to what is required to achieve a very high level of success in this field.

Thus, your philosophy is one of the most valuable components to your becoming a Job Magnet.

You must possess the capacity to easily articulate your philosophy with written and oral proficiency. Your ability to translate your philosophy to others is invaluable. Stringing the right words together at the right time is an art, and is necessary to optimally influence recruiters and hiring managers to give you an opportunity for possible employment.

Let's use another of my personal examples here. Discovering my unique selling advantage was my greatest asset when I decided to switch career fields – from engineering to a position that allowed me to help people; in fact, it was critical. I took a myriad of assessment tests to help me better understand more my unique talents and gifts.

Illuminating Example: I was once asked in an interview why I believed I could do the job without any real work experience.

I responded boldly and frankly (NEVER "frantically" because that would suggest desperation!) "I was born to do this work." This example speaks to innate abilities that I knew I possessed (and you have yours, too!). I gave a strong closing argument that left my interviewer speechless by outlining a variety of attributes that my personality possessed that would allow me to excel in the position like no one else. I also highlighted the extensive training that I financed myself. However, the most convincing aspect of my response was my detailed description of the amount of volunteer hours that I had invested to develop my innate talents into sharpened skills. After this answer to his question, the interviewer felt that I was the only one on earth that could possibly fully succeed in the position! I was offered the job on the spot! – Actually, the interviewer had no choice but to hire me! (Of course, he didn't consciously realize that!)

Homework Activity: Put It In Writing

Develop a statement (consider creating a bullet point list) that best describes your philosophy relative to your target industry. Then, write an essay that describes your philosophy in a format that you could use in a cover letter. Next, give one or more speeches, or teach a class, on your philosophy for your target industry. Also, practice doing several mock interviews with friends and/or colleagues. – Feel free to borrow from the following samples, or use them to stimulate your creative juices.

Sample Points of Industry Philosophy:

- To be a great engineer, you must readily see both the problem and the solution.
- I love working with people because it allows me to learn more about myself.

- I love to sell. It is my way of helping people to solve problems.
- I believe the Human Resource Department is the backbone of any organization.
- I love to organize a project, identify the resources needed, assemble the right team, and then get things done! I like to know that I'm in charge of making things happen.

Sample Cover Letters

Dear Ms. Recruiter,

    I am thrilled at the opportunity to present myself as a candidate for your Project Manager position. I hold a Project Manager Certification from ABC School, and have seven years of experience in management and project coordination. In addition, the position I currently hold requires that I handle logistics for a $10 million dollar project.

    I would love the opportunity to conduct an in-person interview with ABC Engineering firm. I look forward to discussing the needs of your company, and the opportunity for employment as a Project Manager. Attached you will find my resume for your review.

Sincerely,

John Doe

Dear Mr. Recruiter,

    I am thrilled at the opportunity to present myself as a candidate for your Training and Technical Assistant's position. I have a wealth of experience and education in the field of training, event planning, overseeing logistics, and program management.

    I thoroughly enjoy working with people because it allows me to learn more about myself.

    After carefully reviewing your agency's website, I believe that my skill set and my passion for helping families would support the work that your agency provides to the ABC community. In addition, I have volunteered with several community agencies to support community development through family counseling.

I would love the opportunity to conduct an in-person interview with your agency. I look forward to discussing the needs of your agency and the opportunity for employment as a Training and Technical Assistant. Attached you will find my resume for your review.

Sincerely,

Jane Smith

Dear Sales Manager,

I am excited about the opportunity to present myself as a candidate for your Sales Representative position. I am a high energy, goal-oriented, and customer-focused Sales Representative.

I love to sell because it is my way of helping people to solve some of their problems.

I have ten years of experience, a Bachelor's Degree in Business, and a wealth of knowledge in the field of sales and customer service. After carefully reviewing the job description for the Sales Representative position, and talking with one of your in store Sales Representatives (Tony Smith), I believe that my skill set would support the goals of your company. In addition, I have received very favorable recognition in my past roles, which has allowed my sales and communication talents to be acknowledged throughout the district.

I would like the opportunity to interview for the above position at your earliest convenience. Thank you for your attention. I look forward to discussing this opportunity with you in the very near future.

                                                        Best Regards,

                                                        Michael Davis

CHAPTER 6

Step #4: Develop a Resume That Tells a Great Story About You

Your resume is a representation of you and your skill set. It is your black and white commercial. If a recruiter or a hiring manager is not drawn to your resume, they will not consider you for a position. Your resume should give a great account of your professional work experience, your educational track record, associated awards, volunteer efforts, publications, and hobbies and interests.

According to businessinsider.com, Leonardo De Vinci wrote the first professional resume in 1482. In 1500, a traveling Lord in England offered a handwritten letter of introduction to acquaintances, and called it his resume. Resumes have since evolved and become the formal and accepted way that a person introduces himself or herself to a prospective employer. Today, resumes come in a variety of new formats, such as electronic business cards, and websites. The latest trend is the video resume, which is a short clip of the job candidate talking about their professional experiences, and why they would be a good fit for a particular position and/or company.

The Different Types of Resumes

There are several types of resume formats you can use; the most popular formats are <u>Chronological, Combination, Functional, Targeted</u>, and Hybrid. First, the <u>Chronological Resume</u> lists your professional work experience from most current to least current. Second, the <u>Combination Resume</u> lists your skills and experience first, and then your employment history. Third, the <u>Functional Resume</u> lists your professional skills and work experience, as opposed to your chronological history; I recommend this format for you if you are changing your career, or if you have gaps in your employment history. Fourth, the <u>Targeted Resume</u> highlights your work experiences that are related to a specific position.

Often, I recommend using the fifth type of resume, the <u>Hybrid Resume</u>, which is a cross between the <u>Targeted Resume</u> and the <u>Chronological Resume</u>. A <u>Hybrid Resume</u> will allow you to focus on specific jobs, while also showing your professional work experience.

If you have gaps in your resume, you can use the <u>Functional Resume</u>; however, to prevent gaps from happening, I recommend that you start a consulting business when you are between jobs, and also engage in volunteerism within your industry. This will allow you to continue working in your career field while simultaneously gaining new experiences that could attract more employment opportunities. In addition, not only will starting such consulting businesses be interpreted as you showing initiative, but they also may expose you to unique experiences that could be invaluable to your career growth.

You should not have a resume with more than one totally different career field. Having had more than one career field, and one or more short job tenures, are likely to create the appearance that you are unstable and/or flighty. Job Magnets know what field they are in and they stay there – even if they have to become consultants. ***Absolutely, no job-hopping or gaps if you can help it!***

You should consider the following headers as you develop your resume:

Main Header

Your main header should be your formal name, and be at least double the font size of the rest of the text in your resume – to make it stand out in a recruiter's pile of resumes of others.

Contact Information

At a minimum, your contact information should include your best contact phone number, and a professional e-mail account. Your e-mail account may contain your first and last name and maybe an underscore, a period, and possibly one or two numbers. Also, your greeting on your phone's voice mail should sound professional – which means that the listener will hear someone speaking clearly (that is, enunciating well), not using slang words, and using no background music. Your message should be neutral and crisp (that is, to the point, and not long!).

Opening Statement

Your Opening Statement should be a ten to twenty-word summary that introduces you to your prospective employers, outlines your career goals, and highlights your accomplishments. You can also call your Opening Statement your Objective, your Executive Statement, or your Position Statement. Your Opening Statement should be written in a way that grabs the attention of a recruiter or hiring manager, and that keeps their attention for at least sixty seconds. According to an article published in the *Huffington Post*, on average, job recruiters spend just six seconds reviewing the typical resume (according to a new study released by The Ladders, an on-line job search engine).

Professional Work Experience

If you are using a Chronological Resume, your listings under your Professional Work Experience should be listed starting with most recent. With each listing, I recommend that you **embolden** the company's name, but not your title. The reason is that company name recognition is very important because of the weight that they carry in the employment game – basically correlating with value. You might feel that your big company job sucked, but the big company's name on your resume might help you land a job, or at least an interview. Your title should be the second most notable text in your listings – usually one or two font sizes smaller than the company's name, but one or two font sizes larger than the general text of your resume.

Create paragraphs that are four to eight sentences long that summarize each of your work experiences. You can use bullet points – especially if you don't have much work experience. However, I strongly recommend that you consult a resume coach or a good editor if you need help developing your paragraphs and elaborating on your work experience. Remember that *your resume is a story, so make it a good read!*

Use action words to summarize your professional work – words like *facilitated, maximized, managed, developed, propelled, catapulted, created,* and *supervised.* In addition, your work experience should explain not only what you did (or what you do at your current job) at each job, but also how your actions impacted the company for the better. It should also highlight your major accomplishments – preferably in quantifying terms.

Below are some sample *power statements* that will help your resume to better stand out from the crowd, and thus to greatly increase your odds of getting more interviews.

- Spearheaded a $15 million dollar construction project with a 10% under-budget savings.
- Managed 10 staff members on a $200,000 grant project.
- Created and implemented a $30,000 marketing campaign that increased the company's market share by 10%.
- Developed a mentorship program for new hires.
- Conceived, developed, and published a company employee handbook.
- Wrote a computer basic training curriculum, and facilitated company-wide training.
- Improved company sales by 20% within an eight-month period.

Power statements are *not* optional in a great resume; they are **ESSENTIAL!!!** When you w*rite an interesting resume, people will read it!!!*

Education

The information under your Education header should include all of the formal and non-formal training that you have acquired that is relevant to the position and/or career field that you are pursuing. You should include your relevant college degrees, college classes that are particularly relevant to your career direction, certifications, workshops, webinars, and relevant books which have published material and articles of yours.

Your formal education should include your college and university granted degrees, accredited certifications, and licenses.

Your non-formal education should include all of your relevant specialized training in which you did not receive a degree, an accredited certification, or a license. Many people do not list their non-formal education because they believe that employers will not value it; however, the fact is that potential employers *will* value it if it relates to the field(s) in which you are applying.

Realize that – when done expertly – the information under your Education header can *make you look like an expert,* which will set your resume apart from the resumes of the masses. For example, if you are an engineer, then you should have specialized training in the area(s) of engineering in which you want to work. This is the area on your resume that should *emphatically stand out;* it should show that you possess the training necessary to do the job that you are seeking. If you are still in school and/or have a rather high grade point average, you should include those bits of information as well. As mentioned above, remember that *your resume is a story; so fill it with interesting facts about your education that will make recruiters and hiring managers want to know more about you!*

Volunteerism

You will create your Volunteerism header to give readers information about how you contribute to your community, causes that hold particular meaning to you, and the effort to which you will go to make life better for others – in essence, the core of who you are. This is where you show how you donate your time. If you mentored with Big Brothers or Big Sisters, spent time fixing up houses with Habitat for Humanity, read to children at an after-school program, or sang for seniors at retirement homes on the weekend, this is the area in your resume where you highlight those contributions to the community.

Some companies look at your volunteer activities to

determine your "human" side. An article entitled *"Volunteering: How Helping Out Helps You Stand Out In the Workplace,"* featured on *Forbe's* web site in October 2013, pointed out that helping out helps you stand out because companies are looking for well-rounded candidates – specifically "do-gooders" who will ultimately represent them well in the world. In fact (also according to LinkedIn LNKD), one in every five hiring managers in the U.S. says he or she has selected a candidate because of his or her volunteer experience. Why? That kind of work feeds your soul while showcasing your interests; it's a perfect way to illustrate who you are, and what you care about, to potential employers.

Therefore, find a way to integrate volunteerism into your schedule, and highlight it on your resume! However, Important Caveat: Make sure that your volunteer activities genuinely align with your values and your passions because, in an interview, questions may be asked about why you have chosen a particular volunteer effort. And professional interviewers often will "sniff out" a non-genuine response! Bottom line: **Job Magnets give back!!!**

Associations

Under your Association header, you will highlight the professional associations, clubs, fraternities, sororities, civic groups, and other groups with which you are associated. This area of your resume is often used by recruiters and hiring managers as an indication that you are connected to networks that, potentially, you would utilize to spread the impact of their company in the marketplace! Your Associations might also help you get a job because the recruiter or hiring manager might also be a member of one or more of the same organizations as you. In addition, being a part of professional associations shows prospective employees that you are serious about growing in your career.

Publications

Under your Publications header, you will highlight all of the relevant books, articles, and/or blogs that you have written. The huge impact to a reader of your resume is that such publications will make you look like an expert. However, be sure that all of your publications relate directly to the job and the career in which you are seeking employment. Your publications reflect your thoughts and your philosophies. Great publications usually will make you more credible as an expert, and help your resume standout from those of the other job applicants. Getting your articles published in professional journals or association magazines could well be your ticket to Job Magnet stardom!

Resume Length

The length of your resume will be determined by how relevant your information is to those making the hiring decisions in the jobs for which you apply. Basically, if you have held five or six jobs (or whatever the number of relevant jobs you have held), you should include them. The same conclusion applies to your relevant licenses and certifications.

    <u>Perspective.</u> Think of your resume as being a book. If the beginning is good, people likely will read it. And why would anyone read a long resume? <u>Answer:</u> The same reason that people read 652 page books like *"<u>Harry Potter</u>."* – because they are interesting! So, make your resume interesting so that people will read it!!!

Video Resumes

A Video Resume is an alternative to a traditional resume. It is a 60 to 120 second clip of you talking about your qualifications for a job. It is a really clever way to get an interview. In the 1980s, Video Resumes started to be taped, but they did not hit *YouTube* until 2007. More and more, Video Resumes are being used to offset the increase in job hunters and the perceived lack of jobs in the United States. In an article published on *Time*'s website in 2012, writer Victor Luckerson said "A carefully targeted video presentation can show bosses your creativity and dedication. Let the web's culture of sharing help propel your name and brand into the consciousness of employers." A Video Resume can be a great way to introduce yourself to prospective employers. You can find samples of Video Resumes on *YouTube* by typing *"video resume"* into the YouTube search engine.

In March 2014, the *Huffington Post* web site published "Employers eliminated a net total of 322,000 jobs in May, according to recent reports from the Labor department. At the same time, about 350,000 people entered the labor force, pushing the number of unemployed people to 14.5 million.

This means, on average, about 5.7 people were looking for work in May for every available job. That's up from about 5.5 in April and way up from less than two people per job in December 2007, when the recession began."

A Video Resume can help you stand out from the masses. However, in order to be truly effective, you need to consider several things when you design and make your Video Resume. In general, your Video Resume should give prospective employers and recruiters a snap shot of who you are – including your personality. Use the following questions to help judge if your Video Resume or your conventional hard copy resume accurately reflects the real YOU! Also, have at least one (preferably more than one) friend answer these questions relative to you and your resume(s)!

- What values, experiences, passions, talents, and qualities constitute your brand?
- What are your gifts?
- What qualities make you special – especially in the eyes of prospective employers and recruiters?
- What is your unique selling advantage?
- How do your body, mind, and soul respond to the typical work environment?
- Are you outgoing, a self-starter, a team player, an analytical thinker, or process-driven?

Do not get frustrated if it takes multiple tries to reach "perfection." Your Video Resume should be brief, to the point, and only about one to two minutes long. Be sure that you dress professionally – exactly as you would for a face-to-face interview. Start by introducing yourself. Then, state the position for which you are applying. Next, be absolutely certain that you clearly and concisely express what makes you the best candidate for the job. Finally, present a strong close that also includes a summary of the main two or three points of the first part of your resume.

If you decide to create a Video Resume, first view some samples by typing "video resumes" into a web search engine, or search on *YouTube*. Make sure that your video is targeted for the industry and the job you are seeking, and that it showcases your personality. You can pay a company to produce a professionally shot and edited video, but most computers are sold with editing software that will allow you to produce a great product on your own. On your Video Resume or on your traditional hard copy resume, you can put a link for recruiters, employers, and hiring managers to see your description of your intent for your video.

If you decide to shoot your Video Resume with a camcorder, you may well need some additional tools to create your video, such as a video camera (also known as a camcorder), a sturdy tripod, a stand-alone microphone, a laptop computer, and video editing software. Your video does not have to be extremely high quality – it just needs to be visually clear, and the audio must make it possible for the average listener to understand what you are saying – including good enunciation! Finally, and most importantly, your Video Resume should enthusiastically convey the same messages and information as your hard copy resume.

Homework Activity: Take a GOOD Look

Carefully and closely reread your resume and answer the following questions that are designed to help determine its quality in objective terms. Also, get feedback from one or preferably more friends by having them answer the same questions from their perspective.

- Does my resume look professional?
- Does my resume align with the career field and job(s) that I am pursuing?
- Does my resume represent the great contributions that I have made on my current job and/or career field?
- Does my resume feature industry name brand companies, and/or companies that have one or more industry specialties?
- Is my resume likely to be intriguing to the average employer, recruiter, and hiring manager?
- Will most others outside my field or industry find my resume intriguing?

Work to get feedback from friends and, more importantly, from people in the field in which you are seeking employment. If you or your friends answer "No" to any of these questions, you need to further develop your resume, and maybe even further develop yourself!

Other ways that you can develop your resume include going back to school to receive a relevant degree; completing a relevant certification; participating in a workshop and relevant training; writing and publishing relevant articles about industry norms, issues, or changes; and locating a volunteer project that aligns with your sensitivities and genuine interests. In addition, make sure that you – as well as a friend with "perfect" grammar and great writing skills – check your resume for spelling, grammar, logic, word flow, etc. before you send it out.

A Personal Example

Before applying for a regional training position with a national training company, I spent several years developing my resume. Once I knew what type of position I wanted, I began attending trainings, reading books, writing articles for publications, and gaining professional experiences to make my resume stand out from the masses. With my first job application, I was called the next day. Shortly thereafter, using a virtually identical approach, except that I applied online, I received a call within 20 minutes. Thus, a great resume can get you an interview quickly! On the other hand, a defective or lackluster resume can quickly become a ball of paper headed to the trashcan basketball hoop.

Remember that you are a "Job Magnet." You are not the norm. So, pay no attention to some of the "conventional" job coaches who do not approve of Video Resumes or other job-hunting tactics that I share in this book. That does not mean that the recommendations of these other job coaches do not work at all. It simply means that you are different, and have an unconventional approach to conventional process. Remember:

If you want something different, you have to DO something different!!!

CHAPTER 7

Step #5: Develop Your Network

Your network – if you have one! – is your most important weapon in your journey to becoming a Job Magnet!!! It will make you if you have a great one, but it can break you if you have a bad or nonexistent one!

Your network consists of any one or more groups of people who are connected to you through various types of relationships including, but not limited to, your friends, family, co-workers, business associates, teachers, neighbors, clients, your child's basketball coach or babysitter, your auto mechanic, a friend's girlfriend, and even your former boss. If you think hard as you build your list of those in your network, you may well find that a practically endless number of people share a wealth of knowledge about you, as well as have ready access to a large variety of other invaluable resources; when you properly leverage all of these resources, I predict that you will be amazed at the power you have available – all for the asking!!! A critically important point here is that you see yourself as *a part* of the network, NOT as *the owner* of the network. This means that you must fully embrace the concept that **you will give more to your network than you will receive from it.**

With your great network, you will experience superior success in your job hunting. When you are connected to the right people, you frequently will have information and access to job openings before they are even listed. You will get more interviews, you will have more leverage in the hiring selection process, and you will benefit from further building your number of great references – even if you don't land the job that is available currently!. Your present network, as well as your developing network, give you the ability to reach beyond your own influence and greatly multiply your efforts.

In his book "Never Eat Alone: And Other Secrets to Success, One Relationship at a Time, Keith Ferrazzi wrote "Identify the people in your industries who always seem to be out in front, and use all the relationship skills you've acquired to connect with them. Take them to lunch. Read their newsletters. In fact, read everything you can. Online, there are hundreds of individuals distilling information, analyzing it, and making prognostications. These armchair analysts are the eyes and ears of innovation. Now get online and read, read, read. Subscribe to magazines, buy books, and talk to the smartest people you can find. Eventually, all this knowledge will build on itself, and you'll start making connections others aren't."

It is important to stay in touch with the people in your network, especially when you are *not* in need of something. This way, when you are in need, and you reach out to the people in your network, you won't look like an opportunist. In September 2013, the *Forbes* website published a relevant sentence: "But really, if you only reach out to people during times of career transition, you're wasting a valuable resource for your professional development." To put it into practical terms, you should contact two or three people (more if you can) in your network each week. For example, find out how you can help them achieve one or more of their goals, or schedule a lunch date that will let you catch up on each other's doings. Such efforts and initiatives show that you are an active part of your network, and that you genuinely value staying connected.

Many people erroneously think that a network is made up of associates and acquaintances that you hardly know. Just *NOT* true!!! A good network - one that works well – is made of personal and professional relationships with people that you know because you have shared experiences with them. You stay connected to your network by sharing additional experiences with them, for example, attend birthday parties, baby showers, weddings, religious services, fundraising events, meet-and-greet mixers, golf, helping with a move or painting a house, etc. You must do what you can to help the people in your network, and they will do the same for you!

Think of your network as a safety net that can double as a ladder so that you will be able to climb over walls or be caught if you fall. If you don't have a great network, very likely you are going to have a hard time moving ahead in your career, and an even harder time finding resources when you really need them. If you don't have a great network, you desperately need to start building *RIGHT NOW!!!*

What Type of People Should Be In Your Network?

Imagine yourself as a member of a crew for a competitive rowboat team. Think of the people in your network as your crew in your rowboat. The type of people you want in your boat depends on *how far* you want to go, and *how fast* you want to get there. The people you select for your rowing team should be the same – or very nearly the same – with respect to their mentality, drive, values, background, and commitment as those in your network; in other words, they will assist you with getting where you want to go. The people in your network should be individuals who will push you to be better, challenge you, support you, and expand your horizons. Ultimately, the people in your network should help move you in the direction of your goals, not your fears. You should not feel stuck or limited; rather, if you are on the path to success, you should always feel motivated by the members of your network!

By the way, don't get in a boat that is going in the wrong direction; that would ensure that you would end up in the wrong place. When you hang out with a group of people going in the wrong direction, it is very hard to convince the group to turn around and go in the opposite direction. Instead, it is far easier to choose a different group – one going in the right direction! <u>Bottom Line:</u> Not only can your network help you land a terrific job, but it also can help you land a more rewarding life!

Choose the people in your network as if your life depends on it, because IT DOES!

I can't tell you how important my network has been to my career over the last fifteen years. Before email became the primary way to send resumes, I looked for jobs by faxing my resumes, and carrying them with me everywhere I went. Since I believe in creating "instant networks," whenever I'm out, I make it a point to talk to everyone about *their* goals, and often I even share my own goals. Some people call it being nosy; I call it being inquisitive. I love to ask questions. So, naturally, if I'm looking for a job I, inquire about employment during a five-minute conversation. I ask some people directly about employment, and others I ask indirectly. For example, when I was working in the engineering field, I attended an extensive eight-week design class on a scholarship. While attending this class, I sat next to several individuals and inquired about employment at their companies. Three of the individuals with whom I spoke confirmed that their workplaces were hiring. After handing each person a resume, I received two phone calls the same week, and scheduled formal in-person interviews. On one of the interviews, I was required to complete a design layout assessment. Then, after a twenty-five minute panel interview, one of the interviewers told me "If the manager likes you, then you have the job for sure." Much to my amazement, the gentleman who then entered the room was the same gentleman to whom I had given my resume at the design class! I was hired on the spot! I maintained employment with that company for four years, and made enough money to buy my first home. How's that for developing an instant network?

Homework Activity: Networking

This networking activity will help you get off on the right track on your winding journey. First, make a list of the top ten people you consider to be part of your professional and personal network. Second, beside each person's name, write the number of times you have met with him or her for a meal, or helped him or her on a personal or professional project in the last three months. In addition, write down the last time that you called them just to chat. Third, write the major goals of each person, what sports their kids play, what their spouses do for a living. Also, answer the simple question "Do any of these top 10 people in your network have good employment connections?" If you cannot complete the list and answer the question, then, almost certainly, you are not connected to the members of your professional and personal network!

If you failed the above project, no problem! Just make a commitment to develop your network by reaching out at least once a week to at least one person (and preferably more than one person if you can make the time) in your network, and connect with them via phone, text, Face Book, or e-mail. Then, at least once a month, also attend at least one professional event, or accept at least one invitation to a personal engagement; in addition, "interview" at least one person in your network with just a few questions – which can be as casual as:

> *Kim, what is your major goal for work?*
> *Josh, what sports do your kids play?*
> *What kind of work does your husband/wife do for a living?*
> *Hey, Rick, do you have any employment connections you can share with me?*
> *How can I help you accomplish your goals?*

Make a habit of meeting new people everywhere you go to expand your network. Give and receive contact information with people that you think would add value to your network. Also, remember that **generosity is the quickest way to grow and develop your network!**

What could be more generous, fun, and sincere than breaking bread with your friends in the warm hospitality of your home? What says "I value your friendship and our working relationship" better than communing away from the job? So, host a dinner party at your home a couple of times a year, and invite some old and new acquaintances to a cookout in your backyard. Be diverse in your invitees, including making sure that you invite people with different backgrounds, as well as those with similar backgrounds. That way, the mix of people will help others to more easily make new connections. And, of course, you will be busy creating even stronger connections with everyone in attendance! In other words, **become the person people want to stay connected to by developing better relationships!**

<u>The Important Bottom Line:</u> **Your job success will be determined by how well you develop your network, and how**

well developed you are as a networker!

According to the U.S. Bureau of Labor Statistics, **an astounding 70% of all jobs are found through networking!!!** Thus, if you do not have a well-developed network, it is high time to start developing your professional and personal network by making it your number one priority! As you move forward, think of building (or improving upon) your network and working on your job hunting as a joint and fully interconnected effort; in other words, they are "part and parcel" of each other!

CHAPTER 8

Step #6: Dress for the Response!

The way you dress speaks volumes about your attitudes, your perception of yourself, and who you are. How you dress can tell an interviewer whether or not you are detailed, neat, and clean, and whether you would fit into their company's culture. Thus, the clothing you wear to the interview can either help or hinder you in the interviewing process.

However, instead of "dressing for success" – the common, stereotypic thought, **dress for the response you want to get from prospective interviewers!** Just as the Video Resume is replacing the conventional resume, the expectation of your personal appearance in an interview is also changing! This can be a somewhat complicated, and perhaps a bit confusing, because "the look of success" means different things to different people – depending at least in part on their definition of success. Having said that, your dress should mirror the successful individuals in the career field in which you desire to work. You should not only look presentable, but you should also fit the part of the position for which you are applying. Remember that the way you dress mirrors how you want people to treat you! Your first impression could mean the start day of your new job! Yet another way to look at this is "you only get one chance to make a good first impression!"

Everyday Attire

As a Job Magnet, you should think of yourself as being in a movie in which you have to be "in character" at all times! This means that you should dress for the role you want to play in the career or job you want, and that your wardrobe plays a major part in your job hunting success. If you want a job as a carpenter, you should dress like a carpenter. If you want a job as an engineer, you should dress like an engineer. If you are an artist, you should wear jeans and a shirt that shows off your creativity. When you are looking for a job, you should be ready to interview virtually any time you step out of your house. Your everyday attire should be very neat and clean. Remember, how you dress tells people who you are, and you have no way of knowing when an impromptu interview may present itself to you!

Interview Attire

When you walk into your interview, the interviewer should not know whether you are there for an interview, or if you are one of the board of directors who got lost while walking to the bathroom! When you are preparing to go to an interview, I recommend the following for both men and women.

Clothing:

- Men and women should wear a neatly pressed dark colored suit
- Men should wear a tie, hard bottom dress shoes, and dress socks
- Women should wear appropriate flesh toned pantyhose, dresses and skirts no higher than two inches above the knee, and closed- toe shoes

Jewelry:

- Women should wear stud earrings
- Women should wear no more than one ring or bracelet per hand or arm

Hair/Nails/Body:

- If a man has a beard, it should be neatly trimmed
- Nails should be neat, clean, and professional looking
- For women, French tips, nude tones, or neatly filed nails with no polish or colors
- Hair color should be minimized or eliminated altogether
- Neither men nor women should wear fragrances
- Pull back loose and long hair, including locks
- If possible, cover all tattoos

These recommendations are not meant to hide your personality; but, rather, to streamline your look to minimize potential distractions. Scent, hair, loud clothing, strong fragrances, and too much bare skin can cause "transference," which is what happens when a person interprets something and gives it their personal meaning (which may not match your intent!). Generally, less is best!

The Way You Dress Can Help You Create Trust

The way you dress is one of the biggest communication tools to tell people who you are – based on *their* interpretations. What you wear could make you the next new hire or not. It's that simple. Clothes can inspire or answer questions that the interviewer might not voice.

Do I know you? Can I trust you? Do I believe you? These are some of the questions that people ask themselves subconsciously when they first meet you – based mainly on your outward appearance. I'm sure you have heard the saying "You shouldn't judge a book by its cover," but real people do it all the time! Such judging is an innate, cognitive defense mechanism that tells people what or who to trust, what is dangerous, and even what they like.

In his landmark bestseller, *Blink*, psychologist Malcolm Gladwell describes how we think without thinking, about choices that seem to be made in an instant – in the blink of an eye. Gladwell suggests that we don't actually make conscious decisions about what we like and dislike; rather, we pull old files from our memory and make instantaneous, unconscious decisions. According to Gladwell, you will be judged before you ever speak. Therefore, how you present yourself can make all the difference in the world, especially, in a job interview.

Society tends to confuse most people. Society tells us to be ourselves, and that there are laws in place that allow us to be free to express ourselves, and that protect us from discrimination. However, what society doesn't tell us is that many people will not appreciate our individual expression of who we are, and that there is nothing we can do about it. The reality is that, when you sit down for an interview, you will not know if the person on the other side of the table will trust you, if they will appreciate your self-expressions, or if they will connect with you. However, it is not your job to figure this out *in the interview;* it is your job to make sure that you *minimize* the chances of unnecessary distractions. The way that you dress for an interview is not about being stylish, being a clone, or even a kiss-up; it's about the impression that you want to make. It's about starting off on the right foot and minimizing obstacles. But, most of all, it's about *getting the job!* – Whether you like it or not, how you dress will greatly affect your hiring success, and possibly even the degree of your success and the length of your career!

How You Dress Can Affect How You Feel

It has been proven that what you wear can influence how you feel. On October 24, 2013, on *Forbes.com,* fashion stylist Lindsey Shores wrote "It's been proven that dressing well can increase your income." In addition to increasing your income, Lindsey also maintained that dressing well is also important for your self-respect and your composure. When your clothing fits you well and you look sharp, you feel better about yourself. Your clothing helps to bring you into character, and to support your state of mind. When you put on a business suit, you are more likely to feel like you are ready to do business. When you put on a gym suit, you may feel like working out. And when you put on a pair of overalls, you may feel like doing some home improvement work. When your eyes and your body agree that what you are wearing means you can do something in particular, your mind will automatically follow and create a feeling of success with respect to what you are about to do! Now – to ramp up your consciousness to an even higher level, you can then select how you walk, how you talk, and even how you think! – Let's consider a personal example again.

Several years ago I was coaching a young man who desperately wanted a better job than the one he had. After thoroughly investigating his wardrobe and achieving an understanding of the type of job he was seeking, we selected an outfit for the desired response. We also discussed and analyzed a huge array of other things – from his personal and formal presentation of his qualifications, to wearing collared shirts, the color of his belt, and the type of shoes he should wear. He was sincere about his wants, needs, and his eagerness to advance in his career; therefore, he was open to being developed, and it worked. Not only did this young man get the job, but the recruiter also was asked to find other job candidates that had the same attitude and professionalism as this young man. Furthermore, the recruiter asked me to do several workshops on "Dressing for the Response." Obtaining this job started this young man on a journey toward a rewarding career in the criminal justice field, and also further cemented my belief as to "what it takes to get a job in ninety days!" Skeptics as to the extreme importance of presentation may be swayed to my way of thinking by doing the following activity.

Homework Activity: Dress for Success

Conduct research on how successful individuals dress who work in the career field you desire. Interview several of these individuals, and notice – in detail – what they wear. Then, comment to them on the items you admire the most. This activity will allow you to get up-close and personal examples of how the influential "movers and shakers" dress in the career field you want. Take cues from each person's wardrobe, and add them to your casual and professional clothing inventory. Also, ask questions about why they wear certain types of clothing – both casual and professional. In addition, peruse fashion magazines and visit department stores to become better educated in the latest trends in casual and professional attire. Then, add a few new pieces to your wardrobe!

Finally, if it is financially feasible, get a professional makeover. If finances are limited, ask a friend who has a great sense of professional style to help you create a new, more professional look. If you cannot afford to purchase new interview clothing, borrow or rent appropriate clothing for your interviews, and do lots of window shopping. Also, simply trying on new clothes in stores will help you experience how nice clothing feels on your body, your mind, and your spirit. In addition, window-shopping will give you something to strive to attain.

<u>The Bottom Line:</u> The more effectively you dress, the more you will impress your interviewer!

CHAPTER 9

Step #7: Ace That Interview

The interview is the gateway to your job. It is the major determining factor that tells interviewers whether you have what it takes to perform the job, whether they like you or not, and whether they want to hire you. **Doing well in the interview is an absolute must!!!** A job interview is like an audition: you have to be prepared, be equipped, be yourself, and nail it the very first time!

Before learning how to ace the interview, let's define it. An interview is any engagement with another person that could lead to a job. That's a pretty broad definition of a job interview, right? Exactly! That's because just about everyone we know or speak with daily works for a company that is hiring, knows someone who is hiring, or knows someone that will be hiring in the future. Whether you know it or not, this means that you are interviewing every day, and may not even realize it. Every conversation that you have on a given day could be an interview; and, of course, if you talk with a hiring manager or a recruiter on the phone or in person, that would constitute an interview, too.

How to Get a Job Interview

Believe it or not, getting a job interview is very easy. In order for you to get an interview, you must first put into your mind the concept and the decision that you are now actively and whole-heartedly looking for a job. This means that you must be willing to look under every rock, look around every corner, and be willing to see every conversation with another person as a job interview. Besides, the best job interviews are informal ones because everyone is relaxed and at ease, and has their guard down. And you don't have to submit a resume beforehand. If the interviewer likes you, he or she will ask you for your resume, and then determine how you might fit into their company or organization.

Since, normally, you submit your resume before the job interview, your resume potentially will be used to weed you out, and thus keep you from getting the interview. On the other hand, when people have a chance to really get to know you, you are more likely to be asked for a formal interview as long as you have the minimum qualifications for the job. In addition, if the informal interviewer really likes you, they may be willing to overlook small lacks in qualifications, such as not enough education, training or experience. So, what does all this mean? **Talk to as many people as you can, and always inquire about job leads!**

Even if you are at a family function, ask every adult if they know anyone who is hiring. If you are on public transportation, strike up conversations with those around you – of course, asking if they know companies that are hiring. If you are waiting in the checkout line at the grocery store, do precisely the same thing with those who are standing in line with you. If you are at your child's soccer practice, do precisely the same thing with other parents; however, only ask for job leads if it is appropriate based on your conversation with a given person, and how well the other person is receiving you. No matter where you are, there likely is a potential interview or, at minimum, a job inquiry. Just remember to ask, ask, ask because you just might get a job interview on the spot! If you feel awkward about directly asking about job openings, you may be more comfortable simply making your employment intentions known; although this is not as effective, you can use it as a secondary approach when you do not want to be more assertive or seem intrusive.

If you have a great resume that has vast work experience, then your strong persistence almost certainly will produce formal job interviews. Persistence is the single most important personal characteristic to your getting job interviews. If you don't possess the ability, the tenacity, and the drive to follow up on job leads with in-person visits, phone calls, or emails, then routinely getting job interviews will be almost impossible. **You have to be willing to become a borderline stalker to routinely get job interviews!**

Persistence is how you beat the odds. Persistent people stand out in a crowd because they don't give up; they make it their job to keep coming back until they are asked not to come back, and, even then, they *still* keep coming back! Why? Because they are obsessively persistent! Why? Because they know exactly why they want the job they are pursuing, and they believe that it is already theirs. They keep coming back until someone agrees to meet them. They get interviews that others can't because other people get tired of being told "NO!" Persistent people think that "NO!" is the doorway to "YES!" and they know that if they go through enough rejections, eventually they will get the "YES!" that they seek! – **If you want a job interview, PERSIST, PERSIST, PERSIST!!!**

Getting a formal interview can be a bit more difficult than getting an informal one because the competition is fierce, and so many people are out of work. According to the Bureau of Labor Statistics, there were 13.1 million people out of work in the U.S. in October 2013.

Using Social and Emotional Intelligence

To develop the ability to read your own emotional cues, as well as someone else's, is an invaluable skill. Social Intelligence is your ability to understand what is happening with the relationships around you, and then how to respond accordingly. Emotional Intelligence is your ability to be aware of your own emotions, as well as the emotions of those around you. Both skills are necessary to be the most successful in a job interview.

Let's first take a look at Emotional Intelligence. If you are not aware of what is going on with your own emotions, it is almost impossible for you to accurately read the social cues of others. Realize that you and everyone else all have subconscious beliefs and biases that influence how they interpret other people's actions, and even their own emotions. Your emotions can have a major impact on how you feel about yourself and others. Your emotions are stimulated by your conscious and subconscious thoughts. In turn, these thoughts trigger emotions, which produce chemical reactions in your body that can make you feel very strong about a topic or situation. Furthermore, these chemical reactions can also make you feel out of control – for example, as if you were swaying from one thought to the next.

The other half of Emotional Intelligence is the ability to be aware of the emotions of others. When you are aware of the emotions of others, you will be able to easily connect with them organically – as opposed to making judgments, developing strained communication, and, generally, making your relationships with others more difficult. When you have (or develop) a high level of Emotional Intelligence, you will be very aware of your own emotions, and have the capacity to develop a good relationship with practically anyone, and communicate well with just about everyone.

When you have a high level of Emotional Intelligence, that

will support your Social Intelligence. Your ability to pick up on social cues in personal and professional settings will get you farther than you could ever imagine. Knowing when to laugh at a joke; when to ask the right question or just listen; when to look someone directly in the eye or look away; how firm to make your hand shake; how hard to smile; and when to say "I am not sure" and "let me get back to you on that" are all social indicators that tell other people that you know how to read other people. With high levels of both Social Intelligence and Emotional Intelligence, coupled with your knowledge of social norms and your ability to instantly and appropriately modify and adapt your actions, you will become a rock star amongst the mass of regular interviewees.

Be Prepared for the Interview

Preparation, preparation, preparation – the golden key to having a great interview!

Imagine a boxer going into the ring without training to fight his opponent. What do you think would happen? To say the least, it would be a disaster! Boxers train so that they are well prepared for whatever might come their way in the ring. Just like a boxer, you must be prepared for whatever might come your way in an interview. Too many good job candidates are bad or horrible interviewees because they do not prepare!

To be fully prepared for your job interview, you must understand what you are up against to the greatest extent possible before you enter the interview room. The following list will help you become well prepared for your Job Magnet moment in the interview room.

First, thoroughly conduct research on the company that has the job for which you will be applying well in advance of your interview. This process will include investigating the company's website to determine the company's values, mission, and philosophy. Also, identify their clients; research the number of office locations; the number of employees; the company's leadership and when and where the company was established. You may even be able to ferret out some of the company's current projects from the website. Anything you learn about the company from its website can serve as talking points during an interview.

Second, the day before your interview, identify what you will wear to your interview. Then, be sure to press your suit the night before your interview so that you will not waste time the next morning and will be on time for your interview. Remember to wear a dark suit if you are a man, or, if you are a woman, pants/skirt and a jacket with a white or light colored shirt for a crisp, professional effect. Also make sure that your shoes are clean and polished. Select your accessories – watch, ring, scarf, socks, belt, etc. – and make sure everything fits and looks perfect so that you look your best. Finally, make sure that you are well groomed the day before the interview by getting your hair cut or groomed and your nails trimmed, and shave, if necessary.

Confirm your interview time and location a day or two before your interview. Use MapQuest or input the interview address into your GPS, so that you will know where you are going and how long it will take. If your route has heavy traffic, and/or, if you are not familiar with the area in which the company is located, a dry run may help you be on time to your interview.

Next, print three copies of your resume: one for the interviewer, one for the co-interviewer if there is one, and one for you to refer to during the interview.

If you get nervous during interviews, or you are not the best at interviewing, practice what you would say, how you would sit, and how you would walk into the interview setting. Get a friend (preferably one who has managerial or human resource experience) to help role play. Role play several times until you are comfortable with sitting in front of someone else and talking in detail about yourself, your work experience, your goals, and why the company should hire you.

Make certain that you allot enough time for the interview so that you will not feel rushed – possibly including a pre-interview assessment. Also, the interviewer may run late, or the interview may run longer than you expected because the interviewer wants to take time to get to know you better (which, almost always, would be a very good thing!). Allot about two hours for your interview.

Getting the details right will save you major headaches on the day of the interview, and help you look like a real Job Magnet!

The Different Types of Interviews

You may encounter any of a wide variety of types of interviews. The following list gives you brief definitions of the most commonly used interview techniques.

Traditional Face-to-Face Interview

Traditional interviews, like most interviews, like one-on-one meetings that have face-to-face interactions. In this type of setting, your focus should be on answering questions, making good eye contact, and showing off your wonderful personality.

Panel Interview

A panel interview has multiple interviewers. The number can range from three to about ten interviewers. This type of setting allows you to show off your group presentation skills. Make good eye contact with all of the panelists, but when answering questions, give most of your eye contact to the person who asked you the question. Also, make sure that you connect with all the members on the panel.

Telephone Interview

Many human resources personnel use phone interviews to weed out candidates early on in the selection process. To be prepared for this possibility, you want to make absolutely certain that you have a quiet room at the time of the interview, a hard copy of your resume on hand, a pen and paper, and a pleasant voice. Also, make certain that you have the correct interview time, and be ready to receive the call at least twenty minutes prior to the scheduled appointment.

Group Interview

In a group interview you are interviewed with one or more other candidates. The purpose of this kind of interview is to see how well you work in a team, and how you influence the others. Do not view the other interviewees as rivals; look at them as teammates. Work *with* them, instead of against them, and you will shine!

Lunch/Dinner Interview

The Lunch/Dinner interview is just like a traditional interview except there is food. All of the normal interview rules mentioned above apply; however, several other rules come into play. These include:

- Follow the interviewer in the meal selection, but don't order that expensive cut of steak simply because you are

invited to "choose whatever you want."
- Always use proper dinner and interview etiquette. If you are unsure how to conduct yourself at a formal meal (what fork to use for salad, which spoon to use for soup, etc.), brush up on these important details well in advance of the interview. You might even enlist a knowledgeable person to help you better understand some of the finer points of etiquette.
- Lastly, remember, consume absolutely NO alcohol during an interview. Even if the interviewer decides to have a glass of wine, you must refrain.

Answering Questions

Your ability to answer a couple of key questions can make or break your interview. Below are a few questions you should be prepared to answer.

What are your five-year professional goals?

Employers want to know where you plan on going, how far you have planned into the future, and if your future desires are in line with the company's goals. They find this out by asking about your goals. Have you thought about your work life this way? Have you ever said where you want to be five or ten years from now? Do you have specific, well thought-out plans for getting there? If you don't have any, now is the time to plan.

Can you tell me about yourself?

Employers want to know where you went to school, how many years of experience you have in your career field, what you are passionate about, and, most of all, how you would fit into their company. Only talk about your family and personal activities if the interviewer brings it up or if it is relevant to the discussion. For example, you could say something along the following lines: *Well, ever since I was a young child, I have wanted to work in this field.* Or *When I graduated from college, I got an entry level position at a small Chicago newspaper because it allowed me to learn the business side of publishing; in addition, I gained valuable contacts that I still use to this day.* Or *I worked for a temporary agency in order to work briefly in a variety of companies to expand my knowledge of the different aspects of human resources.*

Can you tell me about your last job?

With this question, the interviewer obviously wants to know your experiences on your last job. When answering this question, you should never talk negatively about ANYBODY, especially your supervisor, your managers, and your co-workers. **Be positive, and focus on your accomplishments, your development, and any awards or commendations that you received.**

Why did you leave your last job?

Here, the interviewer wants to know why you left your last job if things were so rosy. If you left on unfavorable terms, it is best to respond that you wanted to focus on finding a position that was more suitable or challenging for you. Other responses could include: *I had grown as much as the position would allow me; I wanted to seek other opportunities for growth.* Or *I wanted to seek a position that would allow me to travel.* Or *I wanted to seek a management opportunity,* etc.

Can you tell me about a time where you had to overcome a major challenge at work?

Employers want to hear first-hand about how you handle stressful situations, and how you solve problems. This question is designed to help the interviewer understand your problem-solving skills, your ingenuity, and even your integrity. They want to see what you do under pressure, what you are made of, and if you can articulate your response well. They want to see if you are a team player, if you know how to delegate, and if you can read the play. They want to know how you cope when you are overstressed and in a crunch. To answer this question, **you need to focus on situations in which you have prevailed against all odds, and (figuratively or literally!) "turned the impossible into the possible."**

Tell me about your weaknesses. What are your weaknesses?

Usually, this will be a tricky question to answer. Never ever answer this question with an answer that will tarnish your reputation; you will have to create a way to use finesse. For example, choose something that you do obsessively, such as *I like to support any position, fact, or proposal with supporting documentation or figures – that is, things that can be checked and proven. Sometimes this can be tedious or a nuisance to co-workers who have the information I need.* Or *I am too organized. I show up to work early because it gives me time to organize my day, get a jump on reports, or do some research on the internet.* Or *Instead of staying late, I take work home and end up working way too late.* **Although the interviewer is asking you to tell them about a fault, you must turn it into a plus!**

Why should I hire you for this position? / "What if" questions

This is your big opportunity to sell yourself into the job, and close the sale! The interviewer wants to know if you can come present a strong argument as to why they should take a risk on you. It is your job to give them several compelling reasons to hire you. If the job is congruent with you, it should not be hard to create several legitimate reasons why you are the right one for the job, such as: *My skill set seems to be exactly what you are looking for. I have been looking for an opportunity to work on projects such as this for some time now, and I am very passionate about doing this type of work. In light of my extensive experience that is relevant to the position, I believe that I would be a strong asset to your company.* **If you have done a good job in the interview, then your answer to this question should just be confirmation that you are the right candidate for the position!**

Generally, before you answer a question, make sure that you listen very carefully to the question, and repeat the question to the interviewer before you answer. Also, feel free to clarify the interviewer's question if there are any ambiguities. For example, if the interviewer asks you how you might respond to a supervisor asking about the general interaction between you and a co-worker, remember, to repeat the question for clarity, and to create an appropriate response. After repeating the question, you might say *I am not aware of anything that is affecting our job performance.* You want to convey a sense of objectivity, and the fact that – if there are ill feelings – they are not being generated by or through you. Also, be prepared to answer questions relating to different scenarios about how you handled a difficult situation, how you led a team in a crisis, how you dealt with higher management, how you manage projects, and your experience with problem solving. Here are some examples:

Question: ***What would you do if you saw a co-worker stealing or doing something fraudulent?***

Answer: *I would confront my co-worker and asked him or her to discontinue the behavior. I would also ask my co-worker to bring their behavior to the attention of management. If my co-worker did not take the opportunity to communicate their behavior to management, then I would bring it to the attention of the appropriate manager and inform my co-worker of my actions.*

Explanation for your answer: You want to show the interviewer that you have integrity, but that you also want to be fair to your co-worker by giving him/her the opportunity to make management aware of the incident.

Question: ***How would you handle a situation where you were given the position of the lead on a project, and, shortly after receiving the scope of the project and a list of resources, you realized that you would not be able to reasonably complete the project on time due to the lack of resources?*** (Understand that this is a situation question and designed to see how you process and come up with solutions under pressure.)

Answer: *The first thing I would do is hold a brainstorming meeting with the staff that I was assigned to work with on this project. We would then brainstorm to develop ideas to compensate for the lack of time and available resources. I would also inquire of management and leadership to determine if there were any other resources available in the company. I would also allow my team to choose the assignments that they felt they would perform well, and also accomplish under pressure with such a short deadline. In addition, as the lead on the team, I would stress communication, positive feedback, and support for the members of the team. I would also make sure that the team was aware that I would support the completion of this project, and realistically convey to leadership what the team can accomplish in the allotted time frame. After assessing timelines, resources, and the commitment of my team, I would determine whether or not I was capable of completing this project on time. If I felt strongly that the team would not be able to complete the project on time, I would bring this to the attention of my manager.* (This answer conveys that you are going to seriously assess the situation before you make a decision, and that you will not take your team down a dead end road. This question applies to your leadership qualities, and is often used for management positions to test your integrity.)

Ask the Right Question(s)

When you are in an interview, remember that you are both the interviewee and the interviewer, for the interview is a two-way street. The company wants to know if you are the right person for the job, and you want to know if the job and the company are right for you. Some of your questions should come from information you retrieved from the company's web site, and the others should come from a list of things you are looking for in a company. Questions may include: *What would a typical day look like in this position? What other roles and responsibilities come with this position? Who would I report to within the organization? Will there be opportunities for advancement? What type of training does the company offer for this position? What are the hours of this position? What type of benefits does this position offer? When do you plan to have this position filled?*

Follow-Up

After meeting someone in a formal or informal interview, you should **always, always, always follow up with him or her.** Without a follow, up all of your hard work in the interview could be in vain because you did not demonstrate an appropriate appreciation for this encounter. Your follow-up provides the important functions of reminding the interviewer of the meeting, what was said or promised, your true sincerity about what was discussed, and a chance to ask for a time that you can meet again to further discuss the job position. Your follow-up gesture can be by e-mail or hand-written thank you card, and should state how you enjoyed your interview, and how you are looking forward to hearing from the interviewer or human resources in the near future. A hand written thank you card shows that you care. It makes a very positive statement about who you are; it says *I am not like everyone else. Put me on your callback list. I am a Job Magnet. – Hire me before someone else does!* You should also send an e-mail to each person that you meet in your travels because that informal meeting could eventually lead to an invitation to a formal interview.

In my view – without a shadow of doubt – the following is the best example I have ever experienced for acing an interview. I set up a table at my church to sell copies of my previous books, and to give people literature about my coaching services. I was approached by a gentleman who just happened to walk into the church because of the signs outside indicating that the church was having an expo. This gentleman engaged in a casual conversation with me about my services, and then about my professional work experience. He asked a ton of questions, and then said to me *You know, I sit on the board of a non-profit organization that is looking for someone that has your experience and talent. I think you would be a perfect fit for this position.* He then gave me his card, and asked me to send him my resume. He responded back to my email – telling me that the position had not yet been created, so it would be a couple of months before the position would be available. Sure enough, several months later, the HR manager called me for a phone interview. Before I received that phone call, I had researched the company to understand their mission and their goals. Their website contained several videos that spotlighted some of the staff, which I watched in its entirety. In the phone interview, I mentioned the company's goals and how my goals aligned with theirs. I also mentioned their website video I viewed that featured the HR manager who was interviewing me on the phone. I told her what a great job I thought she had done in explaining the organization's mission. The phone interview went well, and I was invited in for a formal panel interview.

Before the day of the interview, I discovered that there was only metered parking on the street of their headquarters, and that I was going to have to arrive a whole hour early just to make sure that I would secure a parking spot. In addition, I did a dry run to be certain that I knew exactly where the company was located.

On the day of the interview, I arrived wearing a neat, pressed, dark blue suit, a crisp white shirt, and a distinctive, but conservative, raspberry colored tie. My shoes were buffed and shiny. My locks were neatly pulled back and secured. My facial hair and nails were neatly trimmed. I carried a leather-bound portfolio, which held three hard copies of my resume, a professional grade pen, and notepaper with several questions and talking points written on it. Since I had exercised earlier that morning and gotten plenty of sleep the night before, I was very focused and energized. I arrived fifteen minutes before my scheduled interview time.

Three women, who were sitting at a small round table,

greeted me when I entered the interview room. They included the HR manager, the Executive Director, and a person who held a position similar to the one for which I was interviewing. They greeted me with handshakes and pleasant hellos. They asked a series of questions – from how I handle authority and stressful situations, to my ability to problem-solve in a group. I was also given several scenario questions of the 'What if' kind. (Remember that scenario questions are designed to help the interviewer understand how you would handle specific situations, as well as how your thought processes work.) I answered each question with a poised and detailed response. I then asked a series of questions of my own, which included: *What will be my daily duties? Are there training opportunities?* And *Where are the various office locations?*

After the interview was complete, the ladies assured me that they enjoyed the interview; however, there were a few other candidates that were still to be seen. Immediately after the interview, I sent each panelist a hand written thank you card. Two weeks later, I received a phone call from the HR manager informing me that I was not selected for the job. To put it mildly, I was surprised; but here is where serendipity came into play. I had followed all the rules, dotted all the I's and crossed all the T's. I had presented myself like the Job Magnet that I was. However, I was not the particular Job Magnet for that particular position. This happened for a reason. One week later, the hiring manager phoned me; she was so excited that I could barely understand what she was saying. She told me about a new position that she felt I was destined for, and she wanted me to interview for it immediately. The gentleman who had been hired for the job for which I had applied was the person who interviewed me. Although I went through the interviewing process, it clearly was just a formality. Two days later, I was made an official offer and I took the job.

All together, I had four interviews before I received this position. There was the informal interview at the church expo, the preliminary phone interview, the three-person panel interview, and, finally, what I call the formality interview. I passed all four of the job interviews, landing me a position that added greatly to my work experience, and contributed new skills to my resume!

Homework Activity: Interview Skills

Let's do an activity that will increase your interviewing skills and also boost your confidence as a Job Magnet.

Conduct a mock interview with a friend who holds a position as a manager – preferably a Human Resource specialist, but a willing friend will suffice. Ask the interviewer to grade the quality of your interview, give constructive criticism, and make the questions as real as possible. You can even record your interview so that you can see how you respond when you are asked various questions and how you recall facts about past events. If you struggle in the mock interview, you may want to consider hiring a coach to make sure that you are fully on your A game. Since the interview process is so important, hiring a coach would be worth every penny if it improved your interviewing skills. You can also conduct an interview with yourself in the mirror.

You can ask yourself the interview questions, and then answer them as you look at yourself in the mirror. This method will allow you to see your body language. Before you start your mirror interview, take sixty seconds to look into your eyes and concentrate on what others see; then write down your thoughts and feelings. What did you write down? If you were honest with yourself, whatever you wrote down is likely what others will see in you when you interview. If you don't like what you see, work on your confidence with some positive self-talk. That's right, **talk to yourself!** For example, tell yourself how great you are, how smart you are, and how nice you look. Shout out if you are a genius! It works!!! **Engage in self-talking for two minutes straight without looking away, and watch your confidence soar!** What do you have to lose? You can also read a book or take a class on Social and Emotional Intelligence. I can't stress this one enough; it is **THAT IMPORTANT!!!**

CHAPTER 10

The 90-Day Game Plan

When two opposing forces meet – whether it's in battle or in a sporting event, the army or the team that usually wins is the one with the best game plan, the most passion and the greatest commitment to victory.

The 90-Day Game Plan is a strategic action plan that guides you as you implement all of the great ideas in this book. Remember that success is not about wanting something or having good intentions, it is ALL about proper planning, optimum execution and stellar commitment! If you have read this entire book, you are committed, so it is now time to execute! So, commit yourself to do all that you can to become a Job Magnet. Commit to executing the activities in this book in the proper time frame. Commit to working your hardest to overcome any obstacles that stand in your way – **even if that obstacle is YOU!** When you believe that you will have the job you want, you will! Have faith, and take action in the right direction even when you cannot clearly see how it will unfold. **When you believe in yourself, and believe that you have a purpose to fulfill, you will be successful!**

You do not have to execute everything in the order listed below to get results. You may already have completed some of the smaller action items, and therefore can move on to the bigger action items. It is now time to take action and GET YOUR JOB IN 90 DAYS!

Days 1-15

- Start a workout regimen so that you can stay energized, upbeat and positive
- Write a Job Vision Statement
- Identify a career field that interests you and that you believe you would do exceptionally well in
- Take a minimum of three assessment tests: personality, temperament, career, etc.
- Based on your personality, work experience, and innate abilities, ask a minimum of three friends what career(s) they think is(are) likely to be good for you
- Make sure that you have all of the proper attire:
  - If your industry requires a suit, make sure that you have at least one nice dark-colored suit that is pressed and ready to go – including the appropriate accessories. (See Step #6: Dressing for the Response)
- Identify 3 to 5 companies with which you would like to find employment
- Develop a great resume that has a great story about you
- If there is any education that you believe would increase your chances of finding employment in your chosen career field, enroll for it. Enroll in any course, or any certification, licensing, or training program that likely would make you stand out to employers in your chosen career field
- Purchase a pack of blank thank you cards to send out after each interview
- Develop a generic cover letter that can be altered to fit each job application

- Purchase a leather portfolio – or a portfolio that looks like it is made of leather – to hold your resume and pens
- Establish a professional email address, such as smithjohn@gmail.com
- Change all of your voicemail greetings to ensure that they sound professional – with absolutely no background music!

<u>Days 15-30</u>

- Start volunteering with organizations whose missions are aligned with your beliefs, interests, and passions
- Compose a list of the perks, benefits, and qualities that your ideal job would have
- Highlight or underline the "must-haves" on your list – for example, healthcare benefits, work from home flexibility, travel, training, mentorship programs, upward mobility, etc.
- Research multiple companies that have positions with the options that you want
- Narrow your list down to three companies
- In two or three sentences, write a vision statement that summarizes the job you want – for example, a vision statement states what kind of job you would like to have; it should be written in the present tense, for example, *I work in a fulfilling sales job making $85,000 a year with great benefits. My job allows me to travel 30% of the time and it also allows autonomy over my own time.*

<u>Days 30-45</u>

- Develop a resume and a generic Cover Letter that are congruent with the career and position that you want

- Write down a list of all the people you know who trust you, respect you, and would promote you if given the opportunity
- Start communicating with your network about the type of job you're looking for, and forward to them your resume and your generic Cover Letter for them to distribute to their channels
- Create a Video Resume that highlights your work experience, your education, and your personality

Day 45-90

- Continue your exercise plan and stay positive
- Apply for the positions at the three top companies that you have identified as your primary employment choices
- Attend as many networking functions as you possibly can – especially ones held by associations in your career field
- Send out at least 20 resumes and/or apply for at least 20 jobs per week (This is a numbers game. Therefore, in order to increase your odds of connecting with the right person for your resume, you must "prime the pump." Apply for 20 jobs even if they are not with your three primary companies. The purpose of this is to create momentum. The more energy you put out, the more you will get in return.)
- Every day, talk with 2 to 3 people who you know personally until you exhaust your contact list
- Create opportunities to conduct one or two informal interviews every day. Talk to people when you're in the grocery store, the library, on public transportation, picking up your child from daycare, etc.

- Attend conferences that focus on your career field
- Update your Social Media profiles, and use them to start making new connections and inquiring about job leads
- Practice conducting mock interviews

Again, you may have already conducted some of these activities, and not all of these activities are guaranteed to be relevant to you and your situation. This action plan just helps to keep you on track as it pertains to getting your job in 90 days. Remember to stay committed to the numbers; in due time, everything else will work out.

CHAPTER 11

So You Want to be a Job Magnet?

After reading this book in its entirety, you should have a good understanding of how to get a job. Now, in order to become a true Job Magnet, you must not only faithfully follow each step, but also present the confidence it takes to become a Job Magnet. Only when you have achieved both of these objectives will jobs start falling in your lap. Note that getting a job in 90 days is not becoming a Job Magnet; it just means you got a job in 90 days. To become a Job Magnet, you must embrace the Job Magnet Philosophy to the fullest, produce quality work, be an outstanding employee, and have high levels of Social and Emotional Intelligence. By whole-heartedly following each step and completing all of the exercises in this book, it will still take time for you to become a Job Magnet. Understand that a Job Magnet is not born overnight; rather, he or she is developed over time.

The biography *End Game* tells the story of how, at the young age of sixteen, Bobby Fisher became the youngest chess master in history. Many people thought Fisher was an overnight sensation, but that is not true. Starting at age six, Bobby Fisher studied and played against some of the greatest players for ten years before he became a master. If you want to become a full-fledged Job Magnet, you must be willing to dedicate a minimum of four to five years in one career field, and be totally dedicated to the process – including being committed to the work of studying and working with the best. You must put into action what you have learned in this book to realize not only your full potential, but also your ability to reach your goals. With what you know now, you have the responsibility to become a mighty Job Magnet!

I pray that this book has been helpful to you on your employment journey, and that it will help you develop your career in an expansive and totally fulfilling way. If you desire more assistance, you can contact me for coaching or training by visiting my web site at www.howtogetajobin90days.net or www.therelationshipengineer.com.

ABOUT THE AUTHOR

CJ Gross

I have held several job titles in my working career, but none fit me as well as the title that I use in my consulting business, "The Relationship Engineer." No other title describes what I do better than this title. I am a certified Life Coach, a Certified Keirsey Temperament professional, a certified trainer, and a certified Social and Emotional Intelligence Coach. I am also working on a degree in Organizational Management from Ashford University. I have over ten years of experience coaching and training in the areas of Parenting, Workforce Development, Leadership,

Team Building, and Social and Emotional Intelligence and Temperament theory. I provide training to government agencies, nonprofit agencies, and private companies.

I am the author of *The Parent Connection: 20 Principles for Strong Parenting; Seeds of Greatness;* and *15 Seeds to Plant for Harvesting Your Greatness*. I am also a motivational keynote speaker, and a single father of two lovely girls. I have held jobs in three main career fields, including engineering, social services, and now a very rewarding career in sales. I hope that the techniques that I have shared with you in this book – techniques that I have used to secure many of my positions in each career field – will help you along *your* career journey.

www.ingramcontent.com/pod-product-compliance
Lightning Source LLC
Chambersburg PA
CBHW031925240526
45464CB00022B/946